THE

DARK

BETWEEN

STARS

Also by Atticus
Love Her Wild

THE

DARK

BETWEEN

STARS

ATTICUS

poems

ATRIA PAPERBACK

New York London Toronto Sydney New Delhi

ATRIA
PAPERBACK

An Imprint of Simon & Schuster, Inc.
1230 Avenue of the Americas
New York, NY 10020

First Atria Paperback edition September 2018

ATRIA PAPERBACK and colophon are trademarks of Simon & Schuster, Inc.

For information about special discounts for bulk purchases, please contact Simon & Schuster Special Sales at 1-866-506-1949 or business@ simonandschuster.com.

The Simon & Schuster Speakers Bureau can bring authors to your live event. For more information or to book an event, contact the Simon & Schuster Speakers Bureau at 1-866-248-3049 or visit our website at www.simonspeakers.com.

Interior design by Amy Trombat

Manufactured in the United States of America

10 9 8 7 6 5 4 3 2 1

Library of Congress Cataloging-in-Publication Data
Names: Atticus (Poet), author.
Title: The dark between stars : poems / Atticus.
Description: New York : Atria Books, 2018.
Identifiers: LCCN 2018023859 (print) | LCCN 2018024420 (ebook) |
Subjects: | BISAC: POETRY / General.
Classification: LCC PS3601.T785 (ebook) | LCC PS3601.T785 A6 2018 (print) |
  DDC 811/.6—dc23
LC record available at https://lccn.loc.gov/2018023859

ISBN 978-1-9821-0487-0
ISBN 978-1-9821-0486-3 (pbk)
ISBN 978-1-9821-0488-7 (ebook)

For my mother,
for hiding poetry
where I'd find it.

"I loved you, so I drew these tides of men into my hands and wrote my will across the sky in stars . . ."

—T. E. Lawrence, *Seven Pillars of Wisdom*

THE

DARK

BETWEEN

STARS

STARS

For my part I know nothing with any certainty,
but the sight of the stars makes me dream.

—VINCENT VAN GOGH

He laughed,
my darling
you will never be unloved by me
you are too well tangled in my soul.

I don't know the truth of you
she whispered
but I have that feeling in my stomach
you get before your whole life changes.

Our love happened to us all at once
we had no time to think
we were caught up in the adventure of it
and hadn't a moment to spare.

The first time
I walked in Paris
there was a great remembering
of a thousand different dreams.

I woke before her
and she slept on as the sun rose
spilling light across our bed
she was an angel in my sheets
the girl I would draw
if given a thousand years
and only a promise
she might one day come to life.

THE

PRETTIEST

EYES

SPARKLE

FROM THE

INSIDE

OUT.

She was an endless source of
beautiful ideas and epiphanies
I wanted to live forever
in the quiet inspiration
of her existence.

In the mornings

she taught me French

and after breakfast she would paint

and I would write

and as the spring rain fell on the skylight

and the tea steamed from its mugs

my heart hummed

to the music

of the dream

we'd found.

IT'S ALWAYS SAFE
TO DO NOTHING
WHEN IT RAINS.

There is no safer place I know
than tucked
in a corner
of a café in Paris
with a bottle of rosé
and an afternoon to spare.

To the poet every curve of her was a well-placed word.

A muse
is a love affair
between
art
and souls.

You feel right
to me,
she said,
like naked
on cashmere.

If we were caught

in a snowstorm

in a tent

on the side of a mountain

and things were looking grim

she was the kind of girl

who would smile

bundle close to me

and say something like

Let's sing a Christmas song.

EVERY MOMENT SPENT WITH HER
I BECOME A LITTLE MORE SURE
ANYTHING IS POSSIBLE.

She
was
just
my
kind
of
crazy.

She was one of the rare ones
so effortlessly herself
and the world loved her for it.

Loving him
was like sinking into a warm bath
lying there in the soft safety of his silence.

Her love
happened to me a hundred times at once,
in a thousand different ways,
as a million different colors.

She sipped the air
after the rain
and it tickled
her nose
like sweet
champagne.

She stole my heart
with a lip graze on an earlobe
lingered on a whisper
"don't leave."

Her love came from deep within

a calm acceptance

of who she was in the world

a quiet respect

for the face

she saw

in the mirror.

"Girls,"
the old man said,
"are an ever-flowing music—
no use complaining about the song,
just find one
that makes you want to dance."

Our lovers fascinate us—
we live in perpetual awe
of the particular way they are.

Don't wake her
let her sleep a little longer
tucked beneath
the crimson wool of morning
with only the slight
flicker of her eyelids
left to linger
in her last dreams.

I LOVE YOU MOST IN THAT PLACE

BETWEEN COFFEE AND SLEEP.

She was the dream
I had been searching for,
the one to
wake me up.

Take away
my days
and nights
but leave me forever
mornings
with those
hazel eyes.

My love for her
became the constant
against which I
measured truth.

There are
magnets in my
bones for
the iron
in her blood.

"Well,"
her mother said,
"now you've done it
you've kissed off
more than you can marry."

Twice
I would die
for a little more
once
with you.

The problem with loving crazy
is that crazy starts to rub off.

Sometimes
it's the ones
we only meet
in moments
that stay
with us the longest
never diluted
by the imperfections of reality
but forever perfect
in the quiet fade of memory.

Our love
was not
meant to be
it would stay forever
as unsent letters
dusting
in the quiet basements
of our hearts.

You wore a smile and a scar
in the front seat
of an old Cadillac
we were two kids chasing sunsets
holding on to memories in moments—
all the ways you were
I wish I could've bottled it up
that feeling
drinking it now that
you are gone.

She remained in me
as memories
released at random
as warm nostalgia
or terrible anxiety.

If love could have saved us
we would have lived forever.

It sometimes takes a long time
and a hard time
to realize
he just doesn't deserve your *you*.

She lost
herself
in him
and after
he was gone
there was a great
re-finding.

So many love letters
left on the wind,
that when the trees stir
she sees only him.

Love
the one they are
not the one
they should be.

She burrowed her face
into me,
"I missed you,"
she said,
"*long* before I ever knew you."

Love
by its very nature
is fragile
and that's what makes
true love
so powerful—
you make a fragile thing
strong.

BETWEEN|

HE SHIELDED
HER HEART
LIKE A FLAME
IN A STORM—
HIS BACK
AGAINST
THE WIND.

ATTICUS

140

I love her because she steals my socks
I love her because when I find her in them
they never match
I love her because they are always too big
and the gray part for the heel sits far too high
I love her because she wears them to sleep
and one always falls off
and then she wakes in the night and can't find it
and her foot is cold—
that is why I love her.

I won't ever find the words for you—
you are my everything always
and even that is not enough.

BETWEEN|

You are
my fairy tale
my book
to never finish
let me linger
in your story
a little ever
longer.

"Do you hear that?"
he said,
"Listen close
the universe is singing to us
in shooting stars
daring us to fall in love."

THE DARK

Though my soul may set in darkness,
it will rise in perfect light;
I have loved the stars too fondly
to be fearful of the night.

—SARAH WILLIAMS

There is all sorts of magic
beaming in your bones.

LIFE

IS THE ART

OF FAILING

MAGNIFICENTLY.

The trick is always
to *try*
collect the *tries*
like trophies
and you will
never lose.

"You are a bird,
my girl,"
her father said,
"shake the water from your feathers
spread those mighty wings
and fly."

ATTICUS

We will never get back the life we waste
trying to be normal.

Put your hand on your heart

in you

there is power

there are ideas

no one has ever thought of

there is the strength to love

purely and intensely

and to be loved back

there is the power to make people happy

and to make people laugh

the power to change lives

and futures

don't ever forget that power

and don't ever

give up on it.

It is so easy to forget
we are the same as all the others
in thinking that we are different.

ATTICUS

Have you ever looked at the stars drunk
and sworn they were burning just for you?
It's hard not to believe in magic
it's hard not to believe in whiskey.

The earth was drunk
and it stumbled along
as I walked
steadily home from the bar.

It's a good night for whiskey
there's something about the rain
that makes me want to burn.

"Stay away from trouble,"
momma said
but then
some of us need
the storm to feel safe.

CHAMPAGNE IS A TRADE OF GOOD
TIMES FOR HEADACHES.

Death is the only adventure I have patience for.

I love those laughs
that come from deep within
the kind that are catching to anyone close
that make your stomach hurt
and cry with tears of joy
the kind that come
when you least expect
where the more you try to stop
the harder it becomes
and even when you think of them now
you smile—
those are the laughs
of real old
human magic.

Have you ever
smelled a smell
that brings you
instantly back
to a moment
from your youth?
I always loved that feeling.
I hope that's what death is
just sitting on clouds
smelling old smells.

*The funny thing
about chasing the past
is that most
people
wouldn't know
what to do
if they caught it.*

Down in the cellar were
A hundred dusty bottles
from a hundred different years
We'd open barrels to spill
just enough for a glass
The red would drip down the oak
and with our fingers we'd feel the wood
and the wetness of the wine
and for a moment the world would warm
and we'd know somewhere in that feeling
was life as it was intended.

them wealthier

while they are alive

and the world

worse when they

are dead.

ATTICUS

171

Some days life is a grand adventure,

other days it seems

an uncomfortable necessity between sleeps.

I hate to be alone
there are too many voices talking.

The problem with dating these days
is that we compare real humans
to the perfect potential
of everyone we haven't met yet.

Don't worry
if someone
doesn't love you
sometimes
they are
struggling first
to love themselves.

A soul mate would be great,

but at some point

I'd settle for someone who gets back to text messages.

She loved him with everything she had
but somewhere along the way
she forgot that she too was someone,
she too was worth loving.

I let her go
she was a bird I had caged
that had forgotten how to fly
but dreamed of clouds
when she closed her eyes.

Don't waste any more tomorrows
on someone who wastes your todays.

NEVER

BE AFRAID

TO CHANGE

THE PRINCE'S NAME

IN YOUR

STORY.

You must
let the love
for yourself
set you
free of them.

She had survived
his love
and with the embers
he left behind
she lit the
mighty
flames of
her future.

"Keep your head up,"
the old man said,
"for you are a lion
don't forget that
and neither
will the sheep."

The plane shook
and it scared her
not because she
was scared to fall
but because she cared
so little
if she did.

In all probability
there is a person out there
that is almost exactly the same
as the one you just lost,
except that they are a little bit taller,
a little bit kinder,
and a whole lot better in bed.

She didn't know why she did it,
she felt trapped inside her skin,
and maybe,
she thought,
just maybe,
the cuts would let the light in.

The truth is
sometimes
you can
both
do better.

Sometimes we
feed the hurt
inside us
like a wild bear on a chain
just to see
how angry we can make it
before letting it go.

As he chased demons
born in youth
all I could do was watch
with a jealous curiosity
for the fire he fed with drink
what a marvelous,
inspiring, terrible thing
to live so close
to madness.

We sip the poison
our minds pour
for us
and wonder
why we feel so sick.

She wore a thousand faces
all to hide her own.

She walked
through life
with the eyes
of a wolf
who belonged to no one
but the night.

She was powerful
not because she wasn't scared
but because
she went on so strongly
despite the fear.

Her courage was her crown
and she wore it like a queen.

The bravest thing
she ever did
was to stay alive
each day.

YOU ARE

ENOUGH,

A THOUSAND

TIMES

ENOUGH.

Courage is getting on a bull
knowing no matter how well you ride
you're getting thrown at the end.

We all wear scars—
find someone
who makes yours
feel beautiful.

.

Alone we live short rebellions of death,
together we defy it.

Stay alive,
tomorrow
is there
for those
that wait.

There is not enough time in life

to worry about there not being enough time in life.

There was always
something magic
in the way
she was
in the rain.

"Silly girl,"
the old lady laughed,
"your
different
is
your
beautiful."

*To be alive
is the strange
and wondrous miracle
we forget.*

We are human
bold & brilliant
and we will rise *always*
from the ashes of our doubt
to wield our differences
not as a weakness
but as swords
to take our beauty back.

You are worth your imperfections

you are worth your bad days

you are worth your good

you are worth your confusion

you are worth your insecurities

you are worth fighting for

and you are worth loving.

And that's a fck'ing fact.

The sunset raged

in its gentle fury

a four-horsed apocalypse

charging toward us

huddled on a beach

in woolen blankets

singing songs

on a ukulele

to the ever-riding doom of dark.

As his time dawned
he looked up at death
please he said . . .
"just one more life
I promise I'll be quick."

She was that
wild thing I loved
my dark between stars.

ACKNOWLEDGMENTS

Thank You:

Sarah Cantin

Andrea Barzvi

Spencer Roehre

Poppet Penn

Bryan Adam Castillo

Sierra Lundy

Penni Thow

Joey Parris

David Lingwood

Marissa Daues

Andrew Lutfala

Monarch Publishing

Mom, dad, brothers, and sisters

Lindsay O'Connell

The city of Paris and the town of Giverny

To everyone at Atria Books and Simon & Schuster:

Libby McGuire

Suzanne Donahue

Albert Tang

Amy Trombat

Lisa Sciambra

Mirtha Pena

Lisa Keim

Haley Weaver

William Rhino

Thank You,
xx
Attilus